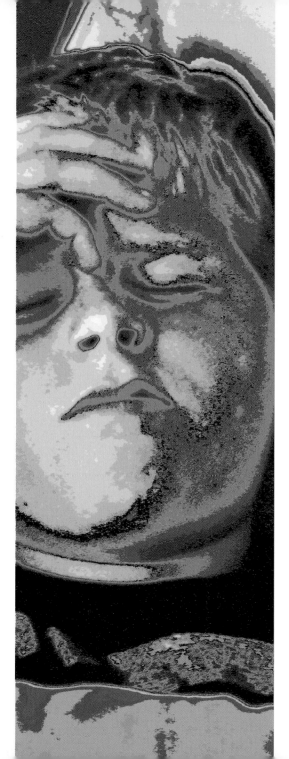

JON DRINKS alcohol

Janine Amos

CHERRYTREE BOOKS

bodymatters
Kate Smokes Cigarettes
Jon Drinks Alcohol
Why Won't Kim Eat?
Is Helen Pregnant?
Alex Does Drugs
Jamal is Overweight

A Cherrytree Book

First published 2002
by Cherrytree Press
327 High Street
Slough
Berkshire
SL1 1TX

© Evans Brothers Limited 2002

British Library Cataloguing in Publication Data

Amos, Janine
Jon drinks alcohol. - (Bodymatters)
1. Alcohol - Juvenile literature 2. Alcoholism
- Juvenile literature 3. Alcohol - Physiological
effect - Juvenile literature
I. Title
362.2'92

ISBN 1842341065

Printed in Hong Kong by Wing King Tong Co Ltd

Acknowledgements
Planning and production: Discovery Books
Editor: Patience Coster
Photographer: David Simson
Designer: Keith Williams
Artwork: Fred van Deelen
Consultant: Dr Gillian Rice

**All the characters appearing in this book
are played by models.**

Picture acknowledgements
The publisher would like to thank
the following for permission to
reproduce their pictures: Corbis 9
(Walter Hodges); Chris Fairclough 5;
Photofusion 28 (Don Gray);
Popperfoto/Reuters 26 (Eric Gaillard).

jon drinks
alcohol

contents

Jon, Josie and Tom are at David's house.

what is

David's parents are out but his big brother Joe is at home. They are listening to CDs when Joe's friends arrive.

'Coming out, Joe?' asks one of the older boys.

'I'm babysitting my brother!' smiles Joe. 'Come in!'

Joe's friends sit down. They have brought some cans of beer.

'You kids can share one!' offers the older boy, whose name is Josh. He hands a can to David.

'We're too young to drink!' says David.

'Chicken!' says Josh, laughing.

Jon doesn't like the older boy laughing at them and he takes the can.

'I'm not bothered. Beer's cool,' says Jon. He opens the beer and gulps some down. It's bitter and he shakes his head. Josie and Tom have some too. They give the can back to Jon and he tries again. Jon doesn't like the taste, but he finishes the beer anyway.

Quite soon Jon feels very

4

Alcohol is a chemical. The type of alcohol found in drinks is called ethyl alcohol or ethanol. It is a strong, colourless liquid. On its own it is too strong for our bodies, so it is mixed with water. There are four main types of alcoholic drinks – wines, beers, spirits and liqueurs. Wines are made from the juice of grapes. Beer and lager are usually made from barley, yeast and hops. Spirits, like whisky and gin, are made from grains such as barley and rye. They are the strongest alcoholic drinks. They are usually served in small amounts and are often mixed with juices or soft drinks. Sometimes spirits are mixed together to make drinks called cocktails. Liqueurs are spirits with added flavourings and sugar.

All alcoholic drinks are drugs. They change the way your body and mind work.

alcohol?

5

warm and a bit dizzy.
He's also excited and talks a lot.
Jon is getting drunk.

Josh gives Jon another can of beer.

'Got to keep up with the big boys!' he jokes.

This time Jon doesn't notice the taste. When he stands up he's even dizzier. He feels relaxed and good about himself.

When it's time to leave, Josie and Tom walk Jon home. He stumbles along, talking and laughing loudly.

'Stop waving your arms about!' says Josie. 'You look daft.'

'And you're talking rubbish – I can't understand what you're saying!' remarks Tom.

Jon thinks everything they say is funny. He talks and giggles all the way home.

When they reach Jon's house, they creep in through the back way. They can hear Jon's parents arguing in the kitchen. Tom and Josie take Jon to his room. He lies down on his bed and closes his eyes.

The whole room seems

Alcohol reaches the brain through the bloodstream.
It affects those parts of the brain controlling speech, memory and balance.

alcohol

The alcohol that Jon has drunk travels to his stomach. In minutes it passes into his bloodstream and begins its way round his body.

When the alcohol reaches his brain, it begins switching off his brain cells one by one. The first types of brain cell to be turned off are those controlling sensible thought, memory and speech. Then the alcohol travels to the part of his brain that controls his sense of balance. This is why Jon has trouble walking and feels dizzy.

'Keeping up with the big boys' is never sensible. Children and young people have smaller bodies than adults, which means they are less able to deal with alcohol. They get drunk more quickly than older, larger people.

to be spinning round.

Soon Jon is spending a lot of his time with Josh and the others.

alcohol in the

They always bring along some cans for him. He pays them back out of his pocket money. He's drinking more and more these days. Jon doesn't mind the taste of beer now. While he's drinking, he feels relaxed and confident.

Sometimes things get out of hand. When they have been drinking, the boys get very noisy. They do things they wouldn't normally do.

One afternoon they help Jon on to a high railing and shout and rattle cans while he walks along the top. It seems funny at the time. They see Tom, Josie and David walking below them. Jon waves.

'Idiots!' says David loudly.

Jon wobbles and slides off. He rips his jacket and grazes his arm.

The next day in school Jon is tired and finds it hard to concentrate. His arm really hurts. He can't even remember now why he was on the railing yesterday.

He feels a bit

8

Alcohol is a poison. Once it is inside us, our bodies work to remove it. This work is done mainly in the liver by chemicals called enzymes. The enzymes break down the alcohol into water and a gas called carbon dioxide. The carbon dioxide passes out of our bodies through our lungs. The water passes out of our bodies as urine.

body

The more often we drink, the more enzymes our bodies make to deal with the alcohol. Our brains also learn what to expect. Jon now drinks more alcohol to get the same effect. His body is getting used to alcohol.

If we drink a lot of alcohol, the nerves that send pain signals to the brain are switched off. We don't feel pain until the effect of the drink has worn

off. In this state, we are more likely to take risks and less able to judge distances, heights and so on. This is why Jon fell off the wall. We are less likely to be able to control our behaviour too. This is the reason that Jon was on the wall in the first place. Getting drunk can be dangerous.

stupid.

9

Underage drinking
There are rules in most countries about children buying alcohol. In France you can drink beer at the age of fourteen, in the UK you must be eighteen to buy alcohol from a shop, and in the USA you must be twenty-one. Shopkeepers and bar-owners who sell alcohol to an underage person are breaking the law.

On Saturday afternoon, Jon meets Tom, Josie and David outside a café in town.

They chat for ages and have a laugh.

'Let's go in for a burger,' suggests Josie at last.

'I can't afford one,' sighs Jon. 'I still owe Josh some money.'

'Come on, you can share ours,' offers Tom.

Over the meal, they tell Jon all about the baseball team they've joined.

'We practise three times a week after school,' says David. Jon thinks it sounds like fun.

'What do you do?' asks Josie, ' – with Josh and the others?'

'Just hang around, I suppose,' answers Jon.

'Hang around drinking!' says Tom. 'Boring!'

Later, Josie, Tom and David set off for the sports centre.

'Come with us!' they say.

Jon thinks about it. He's really enjoyed being with his friends again. But he wants a beer.

'I'll come another time,' he tells them.

'See you,' shrugs Tom.

Jon shoves his hands

harming the body

loss of memory

throat cancer

heart damage

11

liver disease

stomach problems

nerve damage

A small amount of alcohol will not harm our bodies. Most adults who drink are sensible about how much alcohol they have. A little every day can even protect older men and women against heart disease. But too much alcohol over a long period of time can harm anyone's body.

If Jon, Josh and the others continue to drink so much, over the years they risk the sort of damage shown in the picture.

into his pockets and walks away.

On Saturday afternoon, Jon's mum and dad are both out. He asks the boys round to his place.

'Let's have a party!' says Josh. 'Where do your mum and dad keep their drink, Jon?'

'We can't! They'd go mad!' Jon tells him.

'Go on – a drop from each bottle. They'll never notice!' persuades Josh.

Jon and Josh find the strong drinks in a cupboard. They pour some of each into a jug full of lager. Jon passes it round. It tastes awful.

Jon doesn't remember all of what happens next. He does remember crawling to the bathroom and being sick. He remembers crying and asking Josh for help. Now he's in bed with a thumping headache. Sarah, his mum, is sitting next to him. She gives him some water and paracetamol. Jon feels sick, shaky and very ill. He feels like crying.

'We'll talk about this tomorrow,' says Sarah in a serious voice. 'For now, try to get some more sleep.' Jon sinks back on to his bed and groans.

12

a hangover

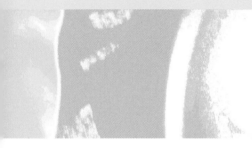

Jon has what is called a hangover.

Your liver can only work at a steady rate to break down the alcohol in your body. It takes about one-and-a-half hours to break down one can of lager, beer or cider, and about an hour to get rid of a small glass of wine or 25ml of spirits. If you drink faster than this, the level of alcohol in your body can build up and become dangerous.

Jon has drunk a lot of alcohol in a very short time. His body cannot cope with it. Messages travelling from the back of his brain to his stomach cause him to be sick. The alcohol causes his body to become short of water, which gives him a bad headache and makes him feel very thirsty. His liver is overworked through dealing with so much alcohol. He feels exhausted.

There is no quick cure for a hangover. It will probably take all night and the whole of the next day for Jon's body to recover.

People say that having a hangover feels like you have been poisoned. That is exactly what has happened.

13

In the evening he has a long chat with Sarah. She tells Jon she is worried about his drinking. It's quite late when Jon finally falls asleep. Phil, his dad, still hasn't come home.

On Monday morning, Jon wakes up early. He hears his parents shouting at each other in the kitchen. Jon goes to find them.

Phil looks awful. Yesterday evening the police arrested him for driving after he had been drinking alcohol. He has been locked up in the police station all night. Phil is angry with everyone. He's angry with himself.

'OK, I made a mistake!' he shouts at Sarah.

'You certainly did!' she shouts back. 'You could have caused an accident! They'll stop you driving and you'll lose your job! How will we manage?' **Phil puts his head in his hands**

14

The police stopped Phil for driving too fast. They found that he had been drinking and took him to the police station. They locked him in a cell. Phil had to stay there until tests showed that the effects of the alcohol had worn off and it was safe for him to drive. Phil has broken the law. He was driving too fast. Also, he had more alcohol in his blood than the law allows for drivers. He will have to wait to find out what will happen to him. He may well be stopped from driving for a while. He may also have to pay some money as a fine. Phil needs to drive at work. The fact that he has been driving while drunk may lose him his job.

drinking and driving

Drinking and driving don't mix. You need to think quickly and clearly to drive safely. The brain receives messages from the eyes; it then sends other messages instructing the muscles to act. The time it takes a person to do this is called his or her reaction time. Alcohol can slow down a person's reaction time by more than 25 per cent.

Drivers also need to judge how far away other cars are and the approximate speed at which everyone is travelling. As alcohol switches off their brain cells, it becomes more difficult for them to do this. Their eyesight may become blurred too. At the same time, alcohol is likely to make them over-confident, take risks and drive faster!

In most countries it is against the law to drive if you have more than a certain amount of alcohol in your body. Some countries allow higher levels than others. If you have been drinking, there is alcohol on your breath, in your blood and in your urine. The police can measure these amounts.

15

Phil doesn't go into work that day. He's worried about being stopped from driving.

He's scared that he'll lose his job. He knows that Sarah is angry with him. He feels that his life is in a mess. He opens a bottle of whisky.

Phil drinks to try to make his sad thoughts go away. Sometimes this works for a while. Today it doesn't. Today the alcohol makes him feel even more sad and hopeless. Phil keeps on drinking.

When Jon comes in from school, Phil is asleep on the sofa. Jon is used to seeing his dad like this. He's used to hearing his parents arguing.

Phil has been drinking heavily since before Jon was born.

alcohol addiction

When people are feeling happy, a little alcohol can help them to relax and make them chatty and outgoing. Alcohol can also make people feel unusually low or angry. By drinking, Phil can sometimes escape from his worries – for a short time. But the problems are still there when the effects of the alcohol have worn off. At other times, the drink only makes his black thoughts blacker.

Alcohol makes the brain release a chemical that gives a burst of good feeling. To get this burst of pleasure, a person must drink again and again. After a time, some people become dependent upon the pleasant feeling the alcohol brings. Their bodies and minds are unable to do without alcohol. They are addicted.

Phil is addicted to alcohol. He carries on drinking even though it is harming him. He doesn't often seem drunk, but he drinks every day to keep up the level of alcohol in his body. He has developed a disease called alcoholism.

Drinking lots of alcohol over many years has put pressure on Phil's body. His liver is overworked. He feels tired a lot of the time. He often has stomach upsets. These things make him cross and irritable. He often shouts at Sarah.

17

After tea, Jon pulls on his jacket. He's going out.

'Be careful, won't you?' warns Sarah.

'I won't be late,' he promises.

The others are at the river as usual. Jon stares into the water. He looks worried. He's thinking about his dad – and he's thinking about alcohol. Josh hands him a bottle.

'Cheer up!' says Josh. 'Get some of this down you!'

Jon looks at the bottle. He reaches out to take it – then he shakes his head.

'That won't change anything,' he tells Josh.

Jon pays back the money he owes Josh. Then he wanders home.

Later, Jon telephones Tom.

'It's about the baseball team,' he tells him. 'Any chance I can join?'

'Sure!' says Tom. 'I'll call round for you tomorrow after school.'

As Jon puts the

the alcohol business

Selling alcohol is big business. Drink companies spend millions of pounds a year on advertising. Huge posters show alcohol linked with a world of adventure. Advertisements on television and in the cinema have people drinking in glamorous settings. They send out the message that drinking alcohol is exciting, cool and harmless.

Alcohol companies are some of the major sponsors of sport worldwide. They provide money for teams and events, and in return their names are advertised on television and in newspapers and magazines. In this way, alcohol is being linked with fitness and popularity.

Alcopops

Alcopops are soft drinks containing alcohol. Their sweet orange, lemonade or cola flavours cover up the taste of the alcohol. Many people believe that easy-to-drink alcopops encourage underage drinking. The makers of these drinks claim that they are aimed at adults only. What do you think?

19

telephone down, he's smiling.

20

Like Jon, Phil has been doing a lot of thinking about alcohol. He goes to the doctor.

'I feel unwell most of the time these days,' he says. 'I have pains in my stomach. I don't eat much and I hardly sleep. I've been stopped for drink driving. I think I've got an alcohol problem. I need to stop drinking – and I'll need help.'

'Let's have a look at you,' says the doctor. She presses Phil's stomach gently. 'Mmm, your liver is a little enlarged,' she tells him. The doctor then checks the palms of Phil's hands. They look very red. This can be a sign of liver disease. She takes a little blood from Phil's arm to test for liver problems. She asks Phil how much alcohol he drinks in a normal day.

'It will take a short while for the results of the tests to come through,' says the doctor. 'But you're right, alcohol is damaging your body.

I'll give you a list of

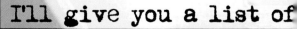

too long

The doctor tests Phil's blood. If he has liver disease, his red blood cells may grow larger. These will show up under a microscope. Lots of alcohol over the years will cause fat to be left in the liver. This can make it swollen and painful. Some people develop a disease called cirrhosis. Their liver becomes scarred and grows hard. One day it may even stop working altogether.

Alcohol may harm the stomach too. Lots of alcohol causes more acid to be produced by the stomach.

This can burn the inside of the stomach and cause pain.

If the doctor finds that Phil has serious stomach problems or liver disease, she may need to send him to hospital for further tests and treatment. Giving up alcohol will be the first step if he is to get better.

Alcohol can be measured in units. One unit equals 10ml of alcohol. Many experts agree that it is safe for adult men to drink three or four units a day. Women are usually smaller and lighter than men. Their bodies work differently and contain less water to mix with the alcohol. Most adult women can drink two or three units a day.

Young people's bodies are still growing. If they are going to drink alcohol at all, it should be well below these amounts.

1 unit: a glass (150ml) of wine, half a pint (250ml) of beer, one measure (25ml) of spirits

4 units: a can of high-strength beer

2.7 units: a small bottle of high-strength alcopop

rganisations with
some telephone numbers to ring.
They'll be able to help you.'

Phil decides to try giving up alcohol straight away.

It's more difficult for him than he would have believed. Quite soon he begins to feel sick and his stomach heaves. He can't settle and he keeps walking up and down the room. Then he begins to sweat and shake. He panics. Sarah makes him a cup of coffee. Phil's hands are shaking so much that he spills it all over the place. At last Phil gives in. He pours himself a whisky.

22

As he suspected, Phil needs help. The next day he telephones one of the numbers the doctor has given him. He fixes up a meeting with a counsellor, who will talk with him about his drinking. Together they will try to work out why Phil has become dependent on alcohol. The counsellor will suggest ways to help him bring his drinking under control. Phil may need to work towards cutting down the amount he drinks.

withdrawal

He may need to stop drinking completely for ever.

The unpleasant feelings that Phil has when he stops drinking are called withdrawal symptoms. His body is missing the alcohol it has been getting for so long. His brain has been used to the switching-off effect of alcohol. Without the alcohol switching off his brain cells, he becomes twitchy and nervous. He shakes. Withdrawal symptoms are strongest for the first three days after giving up alcohol. Some people may need other drugs from their doctor to calm them down during this time.

to cut down on their drinking. They have to face the physical withdrawal symptoms. They also have to cope without the bursts of pleasure their brains have become used to. And after years of drinking, it can feel scary to face the world without the numbing effect of alcohol. Many of these people find they have to give up alcohol altogether. If they have just one drink, they go on to drink more and more to get back the pleasurable feelings they remember. Then they have to face withdrawal all over again.

Group help

There are local groups set up especially for people like Phil. There are also groups that help families or young people whose lives are being affected by alcohol. Alcoholics Anonymous is a group where people who are addicted to alcohol can meet others with the same problem. People who have given up drinking are there to offer help and advice for others who want to give up. Alcoholics Anonymous is a worldwide organisation with more than two million members.

23

symptoms

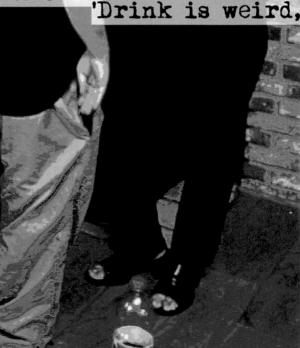

At Christmas, Jon's family has a party.

Jon has invited Tom, Josie and David.

In the middle of the room, Phil is laughing with some of his friends from work. He's been banned from driving for one year, but he's still managing to do his job. He has given up alcohol completely.

'I feel much fitter these days,' he tells his friends. 'No more stomach aches – and I have much more energy!'

Jon is thirsty. He goes over to where the drinks are. Sarah is there, filling up her wine glass.

Jon helps himself to a soft drink. He watches his mum sipping her wine.

back

'Drink is weird,

in control

Drinking alcohol:
- won't solve problems
- won't make you popular
- costs money
- can lead you to take dangerous risks
- can make you less fit

he says.
'How come alcohol is OK for you, but not for Dad?'

'No one really knows,' says Sarah. 'Alcohol isn't like cigarettes. A little alcohol is OK. Most people who drink can stay in control of their drinking. They enjoy the feeling a little alcohol gives them – but they can do without it too. For a few people, like your dad, the alcohol takes control. It takes over their lives.'

'Dad's back in control now, isn't he?' asks Jon.

'He certainly is,' smiles Sarah.

Alcohol and violence

Alcohol can change people's moods. When people are drunk, they may become loud, angry and violent. They can behave in ways in which they wouldn't normally behave. They get out of control.

Crimes like burglary and car theft often happen after drinking alcohol. Fighting at football matches is usually connected with drunkenness. Some football fans have died in fights.

Too much alcohol can cause arguments inside the home too. Men and women may hit each other in a drunken temper. Parents may hurt their children.

Do you know someone with an alcohol problem? They may need help if they do any of the following:

- believe they need to drink in order to have fun
- drink when they are on their own
- drink when they are worried
- drink after an argument or a disappointment
- can remember how last night began – but can't remember getting home
- have trouble concentrating at school or at work because of alcohol
- keep promising to cut down on their drinking but never do – or lie about how much they drink
- always drink faster than anyone else and get drunk without meaning to

If they need help, they should talk to an adult they trust – or contact one of the organisations on page 31 of this book.

It can be hard to say no when everyone else is drinking. Practise saying no with a friend at home – or on your own in front of a mirror. Remember, you don't need alcohol to have a good time. It's OK if you are quiet or can't think of anything funny to say. Everyone is different. Just be yourself. Your friends like you for who you are. It's OK to say no.

Make friends with people who don't drink alcohol. You don't need to drink alcohol to have fun.

'No thanks, I don't want to drink.'
'No thanks, I don't like the taste.'
'No thanks, I don't need alcohol.'

saying no to alcohol

27

Emergency!

If you drink too much all at once, you can become unconscious. You fall into a deep sleep and nothing will wake you. It's dangerous to be left alone because you may be sick and could choke. If someone you know loses consciousness in this way, turn him or her over on one side to prevent choking. Keep him or her warm with a blanket or a coat. Call for an ambulance. Stay with the person until the ambulance arrives.

A large amount of alcohol drunk at one time can kill. It can block the breathing centre in the brain.

If someone you know loses consciousness through drinking too much, turn him or her on to one side to prevent choking.

alcohol

Danger!

Doctors agree that all of the following are dangerous, so **never**:

mix alcohol and other drugs

drink and drive

drink and work machinery

drink and swim

drink and ride a bike

facts

People are more quickly affected by alcohol if they:
- are small and light
- are not used to drinking
- drink fizzy, alcoholic drinks
- drink quickly
- drink without eating

Alcohol is a drug. It can be addictive.

Heavy drinking can cause loss of vitamins, sleep problems, bad breath, stomach upsets, loss of memory and muscle damage. Over years it can lead to liver damage, problems with nerves in the arms and legs, depression, sex problems and some kinds of cancer.

Drinking can make you fat. The liver breaks down alcohol into fat and sugar. One glass of wine or a can of lager has the same number of calories as a thick slice of bread and butter – without the vitamins.

Drinking is expensive. Seven cans of lager cost about as much as a new CD.

Babies born to mothers who drink heavily are more likely to be underweight and have health problems.

In the UK 1,000 young people under the age of fifteen are rushed into hospital each year with alcohol poisoning.

Alcohol is connected with 100,000 deaths in the USA every year.

People who begin drinking before they are fifteen years old have a much greater chance of becoming dependent on alcohol than people who begin drinking as adults.

29

glossary

addicted being so dependent on a drug that you are unwell if you don't take it. Drugs that cause your body to become dependent on them are called addictive drugs.

alcoholism a person suffering from alcoholism becomes dependent on drinking alcohol. Alcoholism is a disease that harms a person's health and can cause him or her to lose their job, home and family.

alcopops sweet, soft drinks containing alcohol. A 330ml alcopop contains about two units of alcohol (as much as a pint of beer or a double measure of whisky).

counsellor a person trained to listen and help people sort out their problems

drugs chemicals that change the way a person's body and mind work

enzymes chemicals made in the body, which speed up certain chemical changes. Enzymes in the liver change harmful substances, such as alcohol, into substances that the body can get rid of safely.

ethanol/ethyl alcohol the alcohol found in alcoholic drinks. It is made from grains, fruits and vegetables. Ethanol slows down activity in the brain.

hangover the after effects of drinking a lot of alcohol in a short period of time. A hangover gives the sufferer a headache and can make him or her feel dizzy or sick.

nerves tiny cords which send messages between the brain and other parts of the body

paracetamol a medicine that stops your body feeling pain for a short time

unit a measurement of alcohol. A unit is an exact amount: one unit = 8g or 10ml of ethanol.

withdrawal symptoms the unpleasant or painful effects of giving up an addictive drug. The withdrawal symptoms of alcohol can include shaking, feelings of panic, worry, sickness, and sometimes fits or frightening visions.

bodymatters

further information

Getting Help

If you have a problem with alcohol, there are people who can help. Talk to an adult you trust, or phone one of the offices listed below. Sometimes the telephone lines are busy. If they are, don't give up – keep trying.

Drinkline

Freephone 0800 9178282
This organisation can put you in touch with a service near where you live.

National Association for Children of Alcoholics

Freephone 0800 289061

Al-Anon Family Groups

020 7403 0888
This organisation provides help for people who are coping with someone else's drinking problem.

ChildLine

Freephone 0800 1111

websites

http://www.alcoholconcern.org.uk
http://www.ncadd.org
http://www.hexnet.co.uk/alanon

31

index

The numbers in **bold** refer to illustrations.

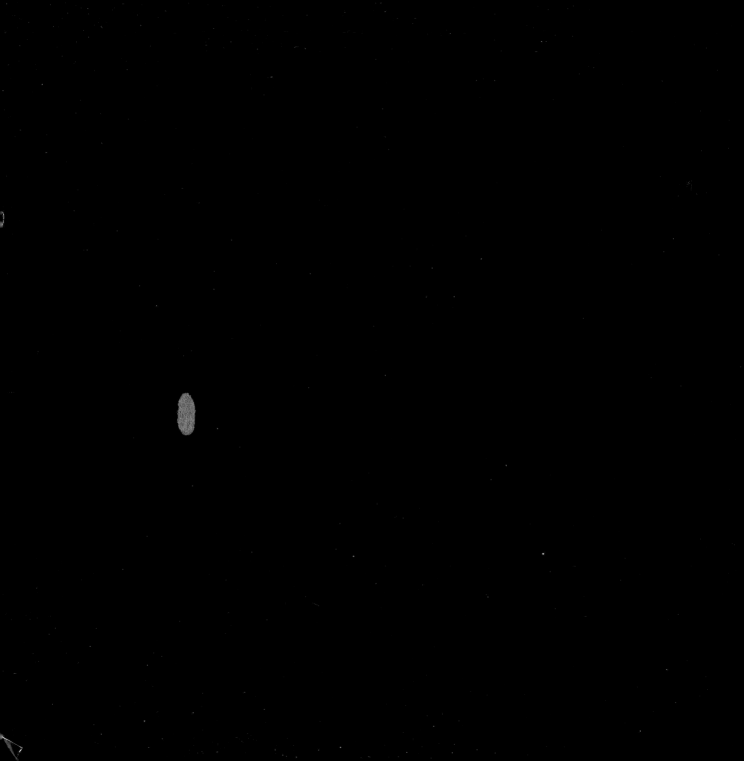